The LAST NOTE Becomes *Its* LISTENER

The **LAST NOTE** **Becomes** Its **LISTENER**

Jeffrey
MORGAN

CONDUIT BOOKS
& EPHEMERA

ISBN: 978-1-7336020-1-3

Published by Conduit Books & Ephemera
788 Osceola Avenue, Saint Paul, Minnesota 55105

www.conduit.org

Cover photos courtesy Scott Bruno and the Library of Congress

CONTENTS

I.

II.

III.

I.

Translation

We love our bodies for their factory qualities,

their two different kinds of beauty: alone

and beside someone.

We love how they texture the dark. If we don't move

for a very long time, we begin to wonder

from where we are disappearing.

On the day my brother inherits me,

there is a double rainbow, which is maybe God's

way of saying I know yesterday

your brother had his first seizure in six months

because I know everything.

Maybe it's His way of gift wrapping

some double parenthetical

in the never ending explanation of love.

Between me and my brother

there is a door. He is on one side

playing Shostakovich. I am on the other,

waiting for a pause

the size of my body I can step through.

When was it even raining?

What are the rules? I shake

his many expensive pills

in their many cheap brown bottles.

I shake the empties to make sure

there are still that many kinds of nothing.

What comes after an archipelago.

What we call silence,

even though it's really just less sound.

My breath cooling as it passes

along the wet of my throat. A note

held so long it begins to fray.

What we don't say when beauty is too obvious.

The Insomniac's Guide to Oblivion

Maybe the space between memories is excessively beautiful

like the space between people you love

who will never move closer to each other.

Let's call this the universe and say it fills the room at night.

You see things that are not there

next to things that are. This is how we feel

about the dead in old pictures

where their clothes are all wrong. We wonder

how long until we are born.

Translation

My brother carries a large window screen into the backyard like falling
    out of love

with the pastoral, like telling afternoon sunlight I know

you don't think of me. I have asked him to do this.

The wasp burrow is beside the compost bin.

No one feels sorry for them, but you have to

wait until night before weighing down the screen,

pouring in dish soap and flooding the nest with a hose.

This is simply prep work.

When a thing gets complicated it stops being a metaphor.

Things got complicated

when my brother came to live with us

and I tried for some time to see him

as both my brother and my son, but couldn't.

My brother negotiates the rectangle of perforated sunlight

like a middle school dance partner—

fear and desire's war of attrition.

I'm trying not to let empathy lead me astray.

He wants to do this correctly,

but is, for reasons no one really understands,

unable to ask for help or direction.

I am, for reasons no one really understands, unable

to accept this, and so I let him lurch

and tottle, saying nothing,

as he pretends to know where he's going,

some inaudible music playing him

towards the lush periphery,

the footpath that snakes down

and then creekside.

I imagine him stopping to rest

where it opens up in the little field

I've named *Beyond Ideas*.

To and from the lip of the hole,

the wasps are like strange drips.

A group of wasps is called a pledge.

I might as well ask the spider

wrapping its catch

above decomposing zucchini

what it knows about behavior therapy.

It's a web he's trying not to catch himself in.

It's a portal he's carrying

and trying to walk through at the same time.

And when I look up he's beside me.

The Insomniac's Guide to Reciprocity

Strike a match to hear the hole it tears in the night, your very own

tiny parenthesis. Let that drip of heat fall towards your fingers

until you remember how soft nothing can be. Strike another.

This is the law of diminishing returns. This is why

fire is not the opposite of emptiness, and why you are not

growing younger no matter how many times you sign your name

like this. The air that is all around you is also

on the opposite side of the world. You dig down

with the same mind you have always had, knowing only more,

and with something less and less like surprise each time

the burn follows you into the dark.

Translation

There's no verb that means to force objectivity on the mutable,

no single adjective to describe how a lager smells

like sawdust and half-gone lilacs. I'm not saying drinking

doesn't help. I'm saying there's no language

in which the phrase "many ominous rain clouds becoming one"

best translates into English as *hearse*. Love is hard enough

and flaccid enough and hard enough again

to assume the pharmacological. Sometimes love is five reds

in front of every rose and forty bucks a dozen.

When my grandfather died, he took the story of our name

with him. Sometimes I think of the dark angels with scissor wings

in Rogier van der Weyden's triptychs taking that story

from grave to grave like wind.

On a train outside Brussels, everything is announced

in English and Flemish and French,

and one either suspects the facts are changing or one knows

the facts are changing, the clouds first pudgy cherubs,

then cloying like silence as the sky sifts,

then something about why one of the stops no longer exists,

or maybe it was a description of its abandoned station,

words trying to mean watching the world grow over

a crumbling structure, the beauty of quickly passing

something that's slowly falling apart.

The Insomniac's Guide to Empty Churches

I like how the pew implies the body

has a listening angle,

how the rows remind you of being

the only person in a boat.

I like the ribbons in the pages

like tongues that must

be abandoned to describe astonishment,

and the narrowness of the central aisle—

its patience and economy dispelled

in the expanse overhead.

The things we say to God

in the rose light and geometries of stained glass

or the darkness of more desperate hours

or both—I like that you only get to be alone

with some of your decisions.

Maybe grace is made of the many

forgotten things and lost parts

of the composite, how you can be

so startled by the guttural

echoing of the wood

as you shift your weight to rise.

Translation

If this town had a mascot, it would be the man

with auditory hallucinations

who hangs out on Eldridge, more specifically

how he makes us look away.

He's so spoken through he's nothing

but mouths and mouths, precipitous

until he shuts them by kissing everything

quiet with a needle's tongue.

Right now he's got the gods sleeping

like lions all around him,

got that good lean going.

I hope it's soft and warm in his invisible wind.

His silence seems to ask:

What have you built with your sadness?

Everybody knows it's easy

to score in this town,

in this country. The canopy of each evening

grows, muffling darkly and blessedly

the day's bright demands.

I watch this man from where I sit

in the fancy beer shop across the street

because I have it on good authority

once you make it

you just have to start faking it all over again.

I'm here to say: I can do that.

I'm here to say: Thank goodness

for the very dark beers

that pour like night, smell of coal smoke

and once inside us smolder, the process

like a fire in reverse. Thank goodness for the train

whistle shrieking and connecting

arriving to leaving, the living to the dead,

even if that means in the municipal style

of a devoted citizen, I'm looking away again.

The Epileptic's Guide to Time Travel

We assume we can tell the future from the past,

as if what the moon does with the water

were mimicked in the blood, and bodies like clocks

could be checked against each other.

We are sure the wind spinning in a tree wasn't born there,

and the flock of small birds carving back

and forth between roofs knows something by vibration.

The last bird knows too much or too little,

stretched from the whole like the tip of a droplet.

If time is a sea, then it has too many surfaces for me

to be this buoyant. Is anything ever another thing's

opposite? Maybe you are people of the future

and expect to be addressed as such. Maybe you never

believed your name was the first fiction, have been waiting

all your life to hear the story before that.

Translation

My brother buys a satellite.

It's an antenna, actually,

but I don't correct him

because it's an aspirational purchase

like when I buy hiking boots or fenugreek.

After a week he returns it. This is how it goes

when you try to haul an idea

over the liminal hills of sleep

and into the visible world.

Let's say the universe is a simulation.

Let's say that when my brother seizes

there are many of him

like bodies in strobe light, the chase scene

in a recurring dream.

He catches and catches and catches

himself: guttural hum and force shut down.

Let's say the universe is benign,

and all the ciphers for love's circular logic

change nothing—

not what we call provenance, not what we deem luck,

not how we parse wish from curse.

Ether, earth, and in-between,

my brother,

we are these erasures spinning above our names

in slightly desperate orbit.

The Bourbon Drinker's Guide to Intimacy

I prefer the contrast of drinking very slowly from a shot glass.

Each sip is immeasurably small, so afterwards

my need is stronger and more invisible.

However you choose to partake, each dead drink

is the husk of a ghost

and also a little empty diving bell

representing the person and the ocean.

It should take a long time, longer than your life,

and you should not walk or speak a lot

as these are the two things that can most betray you.

If you're sitting in a bar, think of the weight of a dart

disappearing in the air, death throes of the jukebox

mistaken for music. If you're at home, make sure every light is on

to muffle the sound of pouring, which invokes distance

and gravity. At home you're responsible, and in the dark it's easy

to confuse the smell lingering in the ditch

with the dead coming back to life.

II.

Metronome

On New Year's Eve my family burns things

about ourselves we want to leave behind

by writing them on thin red slips of paper

and feeding them to candles.

The slips are translucent, delicate as membranes

but also rectangular like fire engines.

I would describe the tone of the ceremony

as twee emergency.

I wonder if the gods are appeased

or aggrieved. The gods are hard to read.

This year I resolved to stop nodding

in the direction of other people's talking.

I resolved to stop personifying winter sky

as "knuckle white" and "the whites of their eyes."

I don't know if this is one of those instances

where if you tell people your wishes

they won't come true

like maybe those who lose weight

and keep it off

are now full of secrets.

I'm willing to risk it.

Mostly, I think this year we'll still be people

who would introduce a virgin

to the bad breath of a volcano

if it meant better harvest,

or even just that the zealots would shut up for a minute.

Anyway, I put a whole fistful of faults into the flame.

I love how they curl libidinously in the heat

like sin putting the moves on hope.

This year I will try again to be a better person.

A Brief History of the Future

I love my wife for her use of indefinite pronouns.

Often she will walk into a room

and ask me if I've seen it.

I have seen the northern lights many times,

but never around here.

I have seen a number of celebrities in person,

but I know she's talking about Jim Jarmusch,

how she saw him without me

in the West Village

and didn't really care except that I did

and so took his picture.

She knows all about the categorical imperative.

I know there are these bonds that vibrate

and when my phone died what died

was that picture, his crazy white hair from behind

like feathers, a dwarf star, that kitschy glowing effect

in movies when a hero wields a magic sword

for the first time. That was the Middle Ages

meaning none of those people had ever seen a sandwich.

I have seen several things that were not there,

but I don't do that anymore. Other times

she will walk into a room as if along a pier or jetty

moving towards the point

where the world as spectacle

and the world as experience meet.

I have seen it.

Wild Quarry

All the empire of nostalgia needs

                    is another person who cares

        too much about birds.

In order to achieve

          a certain American version of dignity,

I pull the hood over my head

             because I don't even know

whose falcon I am

        or what hunting

      today is,
      today is

      a tunnel,
      a tunnel

           for following

my breath around.

        White sky like

the voice of our hoarse Lord.

         Skinny trees like

some ribs the wind discarded.

I think all I want and then some.

I don't know what I want

is the most honest thing I can say

to no one,

moving around the neighborhood

trying but failing

to outflank the divine.

At the top of the list of things

I'm not going to do today,

I'm not going to lie

down in this or that dead garden like a child,

or parrot the word *grave*

a couple hundred times.

Vitamin D

What kind of animal is anger?

Is it when you don't answer

a question

because that question is an order

shaped like a request, gilded like light?

Is it that person

who always has to know who

the "you" is specifically?

What kind of animal is it

when you get mad

at yourself for eating something

or for doing a bad job

pretending

you are having a good time?

I prefer memory,

the variable gravity in dreams,

and these pills

like small orbs of sunlight, necessary

to replace the diffuse efforts

of this our dying star.

You can encourage the animal

to chill out. Put it on a treadmill.

Pet it. Say *sexier*.

In the midst of self-improvement, the animal is less

likely to kill. It's like seeing your boss

at the gym, but your boss doesn't see you

because of the animal.

Three more sets. Two more.

What is the animal when it is many

naked octogenarians in the locker room

falling away from their bones?

In the future we get thin

enough in places, almost winged,

the animal light of the afterlife

shines right through.

These endorphins are like being in a very tall tree

after climbing, near the lightning,

and below so small everything

light can touch.

The Insomniac's Guide to the Small Hours

There's more to falling in love than not getting up.

But how much more? Everything beautiful

is made more beautiful by silence,

and now when I think of myself, the distance

between me and the me in the mirror

is more like time than space, directionless

and untouchable. Night is a nesting doll,

matryoshka, that opens in the middle,

each daughter getting smaller

until the last one

won't birth her successor.

I know her, even though I can't hold her

in my fingers: strange bullet; fat exclamation

point; not death, but a song

about death. I don't need to test

my fingernail along her belly,

or pretend I understand

why she is whole where her mothers cleave,

large seed in night's shallow soil.

She could be solid through her core,

or a hull around a pocket of air

as if frozen in astonishment.

Everything beautiful is made

more beautiful by silence.

Allergy, Theophany

One cloud obscures another like the thimblerigger's shells.

It's the nothing and the waiting, rose quartz

where my eyes should be.

Maybe I'm allergic to looking, the shadow of the tree

steeping and thickening like tea,

lowering itself slowly towards the lake

as if thirsty, one of the many daily, silent recitations of grace.

The body is fighting nothing

and the nothing is winning.

Maybe I'm allergic to the victory, its lightness

becoming itchier and itchier

until every rock and hill seems a holy knuckle,

all branches divine fingers. If the divine is everywhere,

I want to climb down the dark relief

of the tree's shadow.

I want to put my head in the lake. I want the lake

to freeze around me like a halo

in one of those paintings before scientific perspective

where the Madonna is holding the child,

but the child has the unsettling face of a man

and there is something terribly wrong

with their hands, and the field surrounding them

is a small room they will never leave.

Origins of the Roman Empire

You get numb to the pleasure but never the disappointment,

so says the sunlight in August,

filtered through wildfire smoke that hangs

like cloth in a church no one bothers to clean, a ceremony

that may have started already.

This is the month named after Augustus Caesar

who banished his only daughter

Julia to a rocky island for having sex out of wedlock,

chose empire over daughter, dictated his own accomplishments

to be chiseled on his tomb, for whatever reasons

men do that—am I doing that? Probably

Augustus never made his daughter waffles from scratch,

bought the expensive syrup,

stayed home for years, sometimes thought less of himself

in his empire of boredom, how love is about boredom,

how you can turn your back to the sun,

but then your shadow shows up in front of you like a hole

you never stop falling into and crawling out of.

Already today I have unbanished myself

so many times it's like I never left.

Tonight I will sing her favorite song about a fox

that holds in its teeth what the moon helps it find.

Autumn Mannerism

The trees revise their interpretation of burning. I don't have a problem

with it. Maybe if you change every day plot can't find you.

That's where youth goes. It's not time

to pick up my daughter, but I don't have enough time

to go home, so I'm parked in this marginally legal

parking space watching trees shiver in the wind like someone

pressed mute on ominous tremolo.

Sonic nothing, merciful null; I live in one of those towns

where it's easier to beg forgiveness

than ask permission.

Light rain begins to fall

like the baby teeth of something growing larger.

Some kid's grip on the monkey bars slips a little

and he dangles there one-armed.

(Like a leaf, yes.)

There are dozens of children inside that building who know more than me

about how trees sustain themselves, but how many of them

will ever stare at a curated pile of leaves

and try to remember the last time they made a real decision?

No textbook will tell you

fall is the season being in your car feels a little like being in a submarine.

Here I am again in the chrysalis, changing.

The school calendar says tomorrow is chicken pot pie.

The bell is about to ring, and I'm about to be alive.

The Suboptimal Time Machine of Memory

I need to get a bell

for our cat,

so he doesn't kill

any more birds.

My daughter requests

chicken nuggets

shaped like dinosaurs.

This task makes me

feel hypocritical,

but then I remember

my own bell

is simply invisible,

simply not a bell,

and everything is

the long grass

in which I wait

motionless.

It's almost summer,

so we've been talking

about going to the ocean.

This has been

a tough week for no reason

I can name.

The oven timer beeps,

and I think

about shirtless men

at the beach

who fondle

their own navels

as if expecting

such a sound,

as if expecting

to phase out,

Star Trek style.

Maybe they are

just thinking

of youth

like a burn

that won't heal.

A bird lands

at the feeder,

head on a swivel.

My daughter wants

lemonade mixed

with sparkling water.

I remember again

years ago

when the cat opened

his mouth, a bird

flying into the house,

which for a bird must be

the worst part of the forest.

Again my wife assures me

I wasn't there

when this happened.

The Insomniac's Guide to Persistence

If you are paid to sing, you get to call

your voice an instrument,

but most will never know what it means

to be compensated for describing love.

Today the rain seemed not to even fall,

so fine and thin like web.

Now it falls, the percussion of evening

like a large blossom

too heavy for its stem, bowing.

Maybe light turned inside out

is how we see in dreams.

Like holes in a garment, the sky

between branches, wind making the world

seem underwater.

Close your eyes and wait.

The other side of light

hunts west like darkness

across facades and devotion.

Maybe this is what it means

to need more than enough;

the obvious

so obvious it disappears.

The *nigh* in night, the *it* in night.

Maybe this is how you pay the fare.

Blister of want, street lamps sputtering on

irregularly: unlit, unlit, lit, unlit—

votives in the anteroom of sleep

buzz their automated song.

What the Death of the Phone Booth Means to Me

I never really understood what Superman was doing in there.

How did a glass box with a book on a chain help him

remain anonymous? Maybe he liked taking his clothes off

next to our names. Of course, he never got naked.

He had his suit on all the time, underneath the mild mannered one;

cape hidden, its dangling fringe from time to time tickling

the unseen like the lover he never had time for.

The thing is, he was pretending to be human.

His costume was acting like us. And so much of us

involves nonsense that feels good. The delicate positioning

of coins in your fingers and the sounds of them rattling

down in that metal. Remember how in the middle of everything

the phone could ring and ring symbolizing loneliness?

I wonder if he ever faked an emergency, just to call Lois.

I wonder if he ever stood in there feeling untraceable,

loving only the weight of her repeated hellos.

III.

Translation

During sleep paralysis, the mind wakes up inside the frozen body,

as if to ask again the question from an unusual perspective:

Why is there something and not nothing?

I find it comforting to focus on something I love,

which I have no power to change.

I think about Caravaggio's *The Calling of Saint Matthew*.

The burst of light in that painting

enters through the window

as epiphany, but even more specifically

the darkness is lavish and pools like heavy velvet

around the announcement. Inside of what we cannot see, we are free

to imagine ourselves. I have stood before this painting

in the Contarelli Chapel in Rome

as the coin-operated spotlight wound down,

just before the chapel closed for the night: light inside light inside light.

There's also this thing called Stendhal Syndrome,

in which people become physically ill in the presence

of great works of art. Maybe the body is not always ready

to recognize the authority of the mind,

or perhaps the mind even with the body at its disposal

is always and only waiting

for what may or may not be a sign.

Immunity

A little bit of sky gets sucked up into the syringe

with the dead flu.

           It all depends

on your definition of where the sky begins. I've passed out

more than once while blood was being drawn,

but I don't mind

getting shots, or even tattoos. It makes sense to me

that there's a phobic difference

           between addition and subtraction.

Many of our best buildings are shaped like needles.

Perhaps we believe God

is sick.   We are like platelets

           running around trying to stop something, but what?

Sometimes nurses must see in the thin arms of winter trees

           patients they have known.

We take the work home.

           We tell our lovers

and our lovers tell us, our works marry

in the contagion of listening.

The nurse taps the syringe to loose the sky.

The best days are the days you call in sick

even though you are fine.

Translation

The wind is groping trees again. This is what happens

when you fetishize the micro aggression

and side with the maniacs

who argue anything can be a verb.

I don't really feel like dealing with that.

Somewhere down in the deep web,

where night never stops adding

to its enemies list, we do not exist, love,

in the way *Pink Moon* exists for two minutes

and three seconds, or empathy, a competitive eater

named Megatoad, and whoever

first drew the rooster

on the Sriracha hot sauce bottle.

This is a particular moment in history, isn't it?

When people say postmodern, I think

of the Jetsons. Then I hear very distinctly

Nobody from *Dead Man*

ask Johnny Depp's character, William Blake,

"What name were you given at birth, stupid white man?"

I remember graduate school. They kept trying

to build buildings on campus

that looked like the future. I remember Laurie

was still alive. I remember almost nobody knew

who Joe Brainard was, which is probably still true.

I remember Amiri Baraka came to town

and the auditorium was packed and we all looked

at each other like maybe we'd misjudged humanity

in central Pennsylvania. Hope, if it's real,

is a complicated thing that must, for the sake of believability,

appear to be very simple. Like a little personal rain cloud.

Like exes in the eyes of the cartoon dead.

I don't know if I'm interested, anymore, in an image

culled from the pastiche. I don't think I'm interested, love,

in that which coheres and is codified.

It's true, we left you. Boom. Vapor. We left you

for one of those polite, liberal towns we used to make

fun of. It's true. And there we were almost completely.

Even our hands. Even the wind.

You Will Never Get to the Next Level
Until You Stop Doing This One Thing

Autumn light, mute in the bell of a trumpet, soft as junk

when it's good, decorating the shallows we see

but can't quite ford. No one is more

Massachusetts than us, not even childhood,

but I knew I was an adult

when I started washing my hands past the wrists,

could differentiate

several kinds of hysterical

among one or two people

reliably strung out in the food bank.

So what? These are just facts

like a lanyard describes a neck as low-level official

or a chain tethered to a pen

produces a name on a line like a halo hammered flat.

So what? A sufficiently compact mass

can deform spacetime. Maybe you've seen it all,

but see that girl with the capri pants

that don't quite cover

the constellation she is making of herself?

Is she scared crying, withdrawal crying,

or crying like a bird to pierce

the Protestant silence that surrounds us?

Because empire must have everything—

even falling apart—it falls apart.

How many levels is that?

Translation

What kind of prophet would live in a skull ring and never lie

about its inscription, burrowing into the skin

of the pinkie beside the dome of the knuckle

as through middle age the fingers fatten?

The kind of prophet who's not speaking to me.

The way silence seems like trying to decide

how far a tide comes in.

The prophet who lives in this ring

wears an identical ring

inside of which there is another smaller prophet,

and so on

in infinitesimal claustrophobic forever.

He's like my brother

when my brother won't talk.

He's like Prospero except every time he drowns

his book washes back up on shore.

He's like so much shore it's desert.

The prophet taps his ring slowly on a table

to dramatize his boredom.

I want to know what it's like to eat echoes all day.

I want to know if God appreciates it

when we try to surprise Him, even though we can't.

The prophet looks at me and does not say

brutum fulmen,

which means senseless thunderbolt.

Translation

What I love about St. Sebastian is not the colander

the arrows made of his body,

or how he is always shown riddled and tied

to a column, which I should be able to identify

as Doric, Ionic, or Corinthian—

possibly the most pedantic and predictable question

on any art history exam. No. What I love about St. Sebastian

is the painting of him by Mantegna

where he seems to be listening to the sky

the way you or I might listen

to a boss who has no idea what we really do around here.

There is the arrow beneath the right calf

and the arrow through the torso.

Maybe saints are just regular people, only better

at remembering things. If you have a lot of things

to memorize, imagine a building you know well.

You know every room and all the furniture.

Place what you want to remember, for example,

in the fifth drawer of your childhood dresser

below where you have left a picture of each type of column

and all the letters in the word *chiaroscuro*.

Store the arrow there until you need it.

Then you can pull it all the way back to your ear

whenever you want, your body like the dissipating vibrations of a string.

It is especially the last note that becomes its listener.

Caravaggio's Medusa Shield Will Be My Last Tattoo

Painted on an actual shield, his lover in anger and horror screams

for the last time, screams forever: face the disk of a flower,

each petal a snake. The bottom teeth are a little row of tombstones.

Today we might wonder which pronoun the lover prefers.

Stupid hero, *How do you know you're not already frozen?*

I stood on the Uffizi Museum line in Florence for hours.

Stood among however many people who were only there

to see Venus on a clam shell. Stupid heroine,

Your luxurious hair cannot save us.

I wouldn't have waited, for example, for my favorite sculpture,

Michelangelo's Pieta in Saint Peter's, though I love it, too:

the colossal Madonna I always imagine gently laying down Christ

like an exhausted child and walking away,

part Madonna, part Godzilla, a never ending *fuck this*

on her lips. Maybe it's just too sad to wait for,

too much like everything already is.

But I would wait on line every day of my life

to see what I love rendered as protection.

In defiance of my enemies, especially the imaginary ones,

I offer you the emptiness of my forearm

between the deteriorating hinges of elbow and wrist.

The spoils of reflection, the culpability of reflection,

the insignificant difference between men

and what we do. I have been practicing my hiss.

Translation

And in the morning everything's frozen. An irregular breeze
   moves the glistening

mane of a willow like jewels around the neck of a woman

nodding off. And in the middle distance, past hoarfrost

along a chain link fence, a brief line of silver trees—

whatever they are, poplars maybe—like all that's left to prove a ruins.

When you're young you assume desire does something to time

the way chemicals do something to the mind.

And the hateful old men, some of them so young, reliable as moonlight,

when do you become them? In the park

they sell romance, two for five. They pay that plus the angle of repose

beneath giant pines, and the cops go in there the way I go in the refrigerator,

more bored than hungry. My neighbor reports some junkie

stole the flashlight out of his car last night. I'm sorry,

I say, but now I'm thinking of this junkie like a Cyclops in the dark,

without social manners or fear of the gods.

He wasn't smart enough to tie himself to the mast, or maybe

there was no mast, or his arm was the mast

and this is what happened. He points the light. He follows its moon.

He floats towards the song. We all do.

We're not sorry. Whatever, Odysseus. It takes a weirder hero.

Translation

What sort of prophet would live in an axe handle and never think

of a maple tree, its agenda of pollen, how no one sees

the blade as the ass of the thing,

but only as its face smiling politically?

The same one who clears the phlegm from her throat,

uses the words *survival* and *accomplishment*

interchangeably. I'm not feeling this religion, whatever it is.

I want you to know that

my brother and I are only in this fancy camping store

because I screwed up his pills; we're waiting

while the pharmacist portions out tomorrow.

The prophet says, *logs stripped to quarters snap their gossip at the sky.*

The prophet says, *orange tests the edges of domesticity.*

I'm thinking of a book I read as a child,

sight lines across the stream,

the cherry tree felled last year yet flowering.

I'm thinking this axe doesn't have a bone handle without me.

Now you're thinking, the prophet says.

My brother, who's usually not much for social cues,

keeps his distance by pretending

to be interested in a tent the size of a coffin.

Like something dissolving on the tongue,

the prophet whispers, *yes.*

Translation

What's more beautiful than standing in someone's room wondering
   where they are?

A few things. Turning an empty pill bottle on its side

and erecting a tiny ship inside it. Discovering after many years a switch

on a wall in your home that seems to do nothing. Leaving

a third thing to the imagination. There's a point at which I can't go back

to watching people open expensive packages on the internet.

Remember when we were kids, how much quicksand there used to be

on television? This feels like that. It feels as if a new center has opened
   beneath us,

and even our breathing is pulling us down. The ship that isn't real

inside of the bottle that is lists in its ocean of medicinal dust.

And now I am really beginning to notice the effects

of whatever that switch turned off or on. What's interesting about quicksand

is that you have to be so still, have to struggle not to struggle.

What's not interesting about quicksand is that you have to be rescued,

or have to rescue yourself. It's hard to remember

sometimes being left alone is a kind of rescue.

It's come to this: a made bed, a placid sea,

. a bedside lamp waiting like a dim lighthouse

on a bluff above dreams.

All Night No Sleep Now This

Daytime moon. Moon like some guy you grew up with

who won't go away. Moon like God's weird tooth.

Won't go away.

Is impersonating a slice of cake. My stupid heart

blinking like I imagine a button

on a black box does

up until and maybe even after

we have given up trying to remember.

I have given up trying to remember

the train's schedule or the quiet that scatters

from its whistle

like the seed head of a dandelion.

I don't know why it makes me feel better

to imagine a child

blowing pollen across a darkened field.

Up on the moon, my friend lies down

beside the ghost of his wife.

Their bed is a block of ice and soon

they are frozen.

On earth, the terrible things

and the beautiful things

continue to happen beside each other.

On the moon in the darkness, nothing.

On earth in the darkness, sometimes

rain swells like applause.

Translation

How a groove is a prayer for a needle and a hollow

is a prayer for birds, how music fills a space

and makes you aware of emptiness,

somewhere my brother is

not where my brother is

supposed to be. I tell the sky how

and the sky replies in sunlight on the river,

meaning walk the bottom wearing this

and you will know the answer.

I ask the bus dispatcher if she can ask the drivers

to ask the passengers and for once

there is no music to my holding,

just an approximation of silence and nothing

preceded by a click. I am sitting with the phone to my ear

and then I am standing with the phone to my ear

noticing my indentation in the couch disappear

maybe the way things do in my brother's memory.

Now the sky is doing that

thing where it throws some of its light

down in lines like pikes

or stilts as if to say climb up here

and you can see over the trees

all the way to the ocean, the mountains,

so many beautiful places

full of music and nothing and waiting

and you can walk on this river,

sizzling beneath you like a fuse,

sparks of light on the water.

ACKNOWLEDGEMENTS

Grateful acknowledgment is made to all the good people at the following journals in which some of these poems first appeared, sometimes in slightly different forms:

The Adroit Journal: "Wild Quarry"

American Poetry Journal: "The Epileptics Guide to Time Travel"

Anti: "Translation [There's no word]"

Baltimore Review: "Autumnal Mannerism"

BOAAT: "All Night No Sleep Now This"

Copper Nickel: "Immunity," "Translation [What I love]"

cream city review: "A Brief History of the Future"

DIAGRAM: "Origins of the Roman Empire"

Diode: "The Bourbon Drinker's Guide to Intimacy," "The Suboptimal Time Machine of Memory"

Four Way Review: "Translation [How a groove is a prayer]"

Houseguest: "Caravaggio's Medusa Shield Will Be My Last Tattoo," "Translation [What's more beautiful]," "Translation [My brother buys a satellite]," "Vitamin D," "You Will Never Get to the Next Level Until You Stop Doing This One Thing"

iO: A Journal of New American Poetry: "The Insomniac's Guide to Oblivion," "The Insomniac's Guide to Reciprocity,"

The Kenyon Review Online: "Translation [We love our bodies]"

Linebreak: "What the Death of the Phone Booth Means to Me"

The National Poetry Review: "Metronome"

Ninth Letter: "Translation [The wind is groping trees]"

The Paris American: "The Insomniac's Guide to Empty Churches"

Parcel: "Allergy, Theophany"

Poetry Northwest: "Translation [If this town had a mascot]," "Translation [And in the morning]"

Rattle: "Translation [During Sleep Paralysis]"

Sixth Finch: "Translation [My brother carries]"

"Translation [The wind is groping trees]" and "Translation [If this town had a mascot]" also appeared on *Verse Daily.*

"The Bourbon Drinker's Guide to Intimacy" also appeared in the *Small Batch: An Anthology of Bourbon Poetry,* published by *Two of Cups Press.*

ABOUT THE AUTHOR

A native of Fairbanks, Alaska, Jeffrey Morgan now lives in Bellingham, Washington. He is the author of one previous poetry collection, *Crying Shame* (BlazeVOX Books). His works appear regularly in literary magazines like *Copper Nickel, Kenyon Review Online, Poetry Northwest, Rattle,* and many others. He teaches literature and creative writing for American Public University and serves as a Poet-in-the-Schools in Washington state.